GARRISON

CW01044102

ON

ROMAN FRONTIER

by

ROBIN BIRLEY

1st edition 1991
2nd edition 1994

© ROBIN BIRLEY

ISBN 1 873136 02 1

Published by: Roman Army Museum Publications,
Carvoran, Greenhead, Northumberland, via Carlisle, CA6 7JB

Printed by: Colden Offset, Blaydon

Frontispiece: Roman auxiliary and legionary soldiers

Contents

Introduction

The Tyne/Solway isthmus was the base for thousands of Roman soldiers from A.D.80 until the end of the occupation of Britain in the early fifth century. For much of that time they formed the garrison of Rome's northwestern frontier, months of travel away from Rome itself and remote even from the provincial capital in London. In the early years there was plenty of movement amongst the garrison, and a soldier might spend only a few months or years in the region before he was transferred to a distant posting on the Continent. But as the second century wore on, garrisons became more static, and a new recruit might serve his full 25 years in the same fort.

It is evident from both historical sources and archaeology that although there was from time to time serious fighting in the north, those occasions were very rare indeed when considered against a background of more than 300 years of occupation. There was clearly campaigning and serious fighting as Agricola's armies drove through the north and into Scotland, in the years A.D.79-84. The unlucky Ninth Legion suffered casualties in a surprise night attack on its camp somewhere in Scotland, and others must have died in a variety of small scale skirmishes. But Tacitus tells us that Roman casualties were only slight in the crucial battle of Mons Graupius which eventually ended native resistance - some 400 dead, of whom one was an auxiliary prefect, and none were legionaries, the Roman citizens.

Thereafter, demands for troops in more important theatres of war on the Continent denuded the Roman forces in the north, and the frontier was gradually pulled back southwards, until shortly after A.D.100 it lay on the Stanegate road, between Solway and Tyne. Around the time of Hadrian's accession in A.D.117 we hear of further trouble in Britain, and most commentators believe it was probably in the north. At any rate, shortly afterwards the great new frontier of Hadrian's Wall was erected and commissioned, and the troops abandoned their timber forts on the Stanegate and moved into the new stone forts.

Before long, a new Emperor, Antoninus Pius, felt the need to acquire a triumph, and the army spent a few years re-occupying much of the Lowlands of Scotland, building the cheaper Antonine Wall between Firth and Clyde. Near A.D.180, there were further campaigns, but severe damage occurred only in the later A.D.190's, while much of the Roman garrison was absent on the Continent, supporting Albinus in his quest for the purple against Severus. Severus came to Britain with his sons in 208, and much of the damage was repaired, with time for another onslaught in Scotland. But his death, at York in 211, ended the adventures into Scotland, and thereafter Hadrian's Wall was to provide a stable frontier. Much later, in A.D.367, we are told of a treacherous alliance of barbarians against Rome, which apparently resulted in the destruction of the Wall, but we have to suspect that there were few troops there at the time. At any rate, it was repaired once more and re-occupied, until Roman rule collapsed and what remained of the garrison either departed or was left to scratch a subsistence living from the local countryside.

That is the bare story of Rome's army on the northern frontier. But for the officers and men who served in the multitude of auxiliary forces, there was a very different story. Only the minority were serving when major conflict arose, when they could put their professionalism into practice and do the job they were paid to do. It is always the same with standing armies, thank goodness! The secret of success has always been the maintenance of a high standard of discipline and training in long years of peace. Armies usually exist to maintain peace rather than to launch wars, although matters do go awry from time to time. The secret of Rome's dominance for so many centuries lay in the special organisation and training devoted to her armies. It was that which occupied the attention of her garrison in the north.

The Backcloth - The Forts

The life of the garrison was determined both by its forts and the physical environment in which they lay. Clearly that physical environment changed considerably in the course of the 300 year occupation: forests were cut down, roads were driven across moors and through hills, massive forts and villages grew up where little but scrubland once existed, and the sounds of toil in the quarries and mines, with the smoke from lime and charcoal burning, disturbed the natural calm. Individual soldiers may not have noticed many changes in the course of their military service, but the difference between the countryside of A.D.80 and that of A.D.400 must have been significant.

Roman forts also changed in this time. Those of the period A.D.80-125 were built of timber, with turf ramparts topped with wooden palisades: with the construction of Hadrian's Wall, between A.D.122 & 130, the new forts were built in stone. Small at first, civilian settlements grew up outside the fort walls, becoming much larger in the third century and apparently disappearing in the fourth century - perhaps because the civilians joined the soldiers inside the half empty forts. But whether built in timber or in stone, Roman forts had the same plans, and they varied little from one end of the Empire to the other.

The object of a Roman fort was to provide a permanent and tolerably comfortable home for a garrison; it must also be secure from the possibility of surprise attack. There was no question of such forts filling the role later adopted by the great castles, for the Roman army was not trained to fight from a static position. Defences would deter an enemy from a surprise attack, and would also protect the garrison from the attentions of thieves or undesirable civilians. There might be occasions, of course, when the enemy would launch a full scale attack, but unless the garrison was seriously below strength for some reason, or in a woeful state of indiscipline, there would be little to fear for the Roman troops. Something of the sort seems to have happened at Ambleside, however, for a tombstone found there a few years ago gave an unusual insight into garrison life. It recorded the death of a 35 year old record clerk, Flavius Romanus, with the bald statement that he had been killed in the fort by the enemy! If one only knew the details of a few such occasions, one would be able to reconstruct the history of the period much more vividly.

The forts were positioned at tactical points, or at regular intervals along a road. Apart from the obvious motive of wishing to spread the men to the best advantage in dangerous territory, the spacing ensured that auxiliaries drawn from perhaps hostile tribes were kept apart. Thus on the Wall where the concentration was thickest, there were several miles between each fort: not sufficient to keep the men apart all the time, but enough to ensure that they would think twice before visiting each others' quarters.

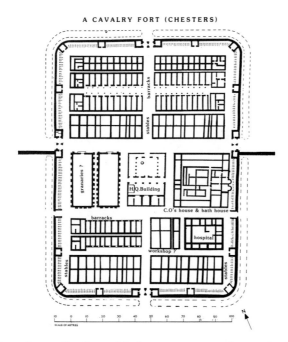

A CAVALRY FORT (CHESTERS)

Plan of a cavalry fort, with three gateways to the north of the Wall.

Within the walls, military discipline was supreme, and the soldiers could not be distracted - except, perhaps, by the sight of officers' wives or personal servants, probably the only women allowed in the fort.

Ditches

Outside the walls of the majority of forts there were ditches, usually some eighteen feet wide and up to nine feet deep, with narrow causeways opposite the gateways. The Wall forts had less cause for ditches than most, since they were protected both by the great Wall itself and its ditch to the north, and by the Vallum to the south, and intruders should have had some difficulty in penetrating the military zone thus

3

created. Even so, traces of ditches have been found at Greatchesters, Housesteads and Carrawburgh, and other forts may have had them as well. More exposed forts placed heavy emphasis upon ditches. Ardoch, north of the Antonine Wall, Whitley Castle on the Alston moors and Risingham beyond the Wall in the Rede valley lay in exposed and dangerous situations, and the series of ditches around the fort walls were silent witnesses to that fact. Other obstacles were sometimes included: pits were dug in the spaces between multiple ditches and carefully covered with branches, to trap the more adventurous natives, whilst thorn hedges or rows of pointed stakes could be inserted into the bank of a ditch. Whatever the particular arrangement, the effect would be to delay an attack, if it ever came, until the garrison could assemble, march out of the gates and engage the enemy in battle.

Where the Wall lay above steep cliffs, as at Crag Lough, the ditch was dispensed with.

Fort Walls

Fort walls were usually between 4 and 5 feet thick, although sometimes greater, and they probably varied in height between 12 and 15 feet to the rampart walk on the inside, with a narrower 5 foot crenellated wall on top of that to protect the sentries. A bank of earth and rubble, or turf and clay, lay against the walls on the inside, adding substantially to their strength against a ram, and allowing access to the rampart-walk in an emergency at any point. Sometimes these rampart banks had ovens or kilns inserted into them since they were the safest places in the forts for a powerful fire, and in the later periods additional fort buildings were sometimes placed against the walls themselves. At Housesteads, near the south-east corner, the fort latrines had been inserted in the rampart mound, and such an arrangement was followed in other forts as well, as at Vindolanda in the third century.

The fine flagged roadway leading from the fort at Vindolanda into the civilian settlement.

Fort Streets

The internal arrangements follow the same general plan, based upon regular systems of streets. Around the inside of the rampart ran the intervallum road, where troops could assemble rapidly from their barracks before marching out of the fort, and where, no doubt, they normally fell in for the daily parades. Four main streets then divided the interior into five blocks. The via principalis ran across the fort, connecting the gates in the side walls. The via praetoria ran from the principal gate to join the via principalis at right angles, dividing into two equal halves the first division of the interior, which was known as the praetentura, the fore-portion. This was assigned to barrack buildings in an infantry fort, whilst a cavalry fort might have one or two stable-blocks within it as well. The via decumana ran from the back gate of the fort, bisecting the rear portion, known as the retentura, which was also used for barrack accommodation. It joined the via quintana at right angles, and this road was parallel to the via principalis, and separated the rear portion from the central range, which consisted of the administrative Headquarters (principia), flanked by the commanding officer's residence (praetorium), granaries (horrea), and perhaps both hospital (valetudinarium) and workshops (fabricae).

The well preserved remains of the east gate at Birdoswald.

These roads were often paved with great flagstones, laid above a solid foundation of rubble and gravel. Sometimes stone bollards were placed on the corners, to prevent the destruction of fort buildings by erratically driven carts. Today these grass covered roads at Housesteads appear broad and spacious, but they were only about twelve feet wide, and when the buildings stood to their full height they would have seemed both narrow and dark. Depending upon the contours of the ground, some roads might have been almost impossible for wheeled traffic - the southern half of the via principalis at Housesteads is a good illustration of this.

Gateways

The Hadrianic gateways were most impressive examples of military architecture. The west gate at Housesteads shows the magnificent masonry that the

Large scale model of a Roman fort (from the Roman Army Museum).
Outside the walls there would be the civilian buildings, temples
and military bath houses.

A legionary detachment in open order, performed by the Ermine Street Guard

7

troops were capable of using, whilst the remains of the Housesteads north gate, or the Birdoswald east gate, still testify to the grandeur of the original structure. Each gateway was flanked by a pair of guard-chambers with doors opening into the double gate-passage of each half, which was closed by huge twin iron-studded doors, not unlike those to be seen today on the Barbican of Alnwick Castle. From these guard-chambers, the duty guards could check the credentials of visitors to the fort, search cart-loads of equipment before they were driven out, and ensure that no soldier could leave the fort without due authority.

Some gateways on the milecastles in the western sector were built with timber, as with this replica at Vindolanda.

In many excavated forts, signs of alterations to the gateways have been found. The great double-portal gates built by the legionary troops in the 120's proved too costly to maintain by the auxiliary troops, and some were soon reduced to a single passage. At Housesteads the east portal of the north gate was blocked before the door pivots had been fitted, but the major alterations occurred much later, perhaps in the fourth century, when many gates were entirely blocked. Although such a procedure might reduce the mobility of the garrison, it undoubtedly alleviated the burdens of the guard roster, which would be essential if there were reduced numbers, and it also reduced the weak point in the defences. At Housesteads even the main east gate had been reduced to a single portal, and the now disused southern guard chamber became a coal store. The west gate was entirely stopped. At Chesters the main west gate was ultimately blocked solid with walls and rubble, whilst the south gate was reduced to a single postern. Birdoswald, Greatchesters, Haltonchesters, Carvoran and Carrawburgh have all produced evidence of similar treatment, and the new fort at Vindolanda, laid out soon after A.D. 200, did not even have guard chambers at its east and south gates, which must have remained closed except in emergencies.

The crenellated fort walls were reinforced by both angle and interval towers, presumably rising several feet higher than the rampart-walk. These served both to give the sentries a greater field of view, and to provide some shelter for their cold and miserable night patrols. Later developments were to involve the construction of ballista platforms on some fort walls.

The Headquarters Building

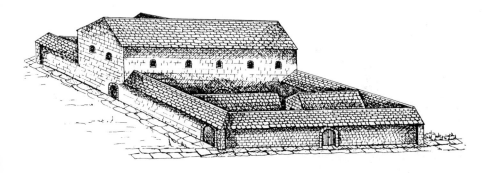

Auxiliary <u>principia</u> or headquarters building, based on that at Vindolanda, designed for a part-mounted cohort 500 strong. A cavalry fort, such as Chesters, would have a substantially larger building.

The most important building within the fort was the Headquarters (principia), lying in the centre and facing the via principalis. As a visitor entered the fort by its main gate, he would walk up the via praetoria and see ahead of him the broad arched entrance of the Headquarters, flanked perhaps by reliefs of Mars and Victory, and with the guarded Chapel of the Standards (aedes) in the centre of its rear range. Some forts,

9

The lonely milestone at Vindolanda - the only survivor still standing to its full height.

The magnificent reconstructed fort gateway at South Shields.

The north gateway at Housesteads milecastle, reduced in width.

The bronze standard or ornamental decoration, found in the settlement at Vindolanda.

such as Haltonchesters and Netherby, had a covered drill-hall or riding school built onto the front of the Headquarters, stretching across the via principalis, for weapon training and drills had to be carried out whatever the weather. Through the archway entrance there was a large courtyard usually open to the skies, but with either a veranda or long low armouries built down each side. From this courtyard another arched doorway led into the great hall (basilica), probably the most imposing structure in the whole fort. In many cases this hall had side doors leading out of the building, through one of which the commanding officer would have rapid access from his house next door. At one end of the hall there would be a raised platform (tribunal), from which the commanding officer or adjutant could issue instructions on formal occasions, or have conferences with his centurions. Perhaps the halls would also be used for small ceremonial parades, and no doubt they were maintained in the highest order of cleanliness. At the back of this hall, running the width of the building, lay five rooms, each with a definite function. To the left, as one faced the rooms, was a pair of offices for the regimental standard-bearers. Here they and their clerks kept the regimental accounts and the troops' savings bank, and from these rooms they issued the pay. The stone screens from the front of these rooms at the fort of Vindolanda had worn grooves at the top, as though generations of hands passing through the iron grill above them in order to receive monies had ground them down. The right hand pair of rooms belonged to the adjutant and his clerks. This was the home of the army paperwork. There would be rows of shelves where the document boxes (capsa) lay, each containing either the rolls of parchment or papyrus or the stacks of wooden tablets, upon which the Roman army recorded the nominal roll for the day, and pay accounts and the character reports of the troops, in duplicate or triplicate. The top of such a document box was found on the floor of the adjutant's room in the Headquarters at Vindolanda. The company clerks might have been envied for their privileges which excused them from general duties and guards, but they must have spent wearying hours copying out dull military records, in cramped offices, under the eyes of the adjutant, or preparing draft letters for the prefect's inspection.

The room in the centre of this range had a very different function. This was the Chapel of the Standards (aedes), the sacred home of the regimental battle-honours and standards, where great altars to a few select Roman gods would stand, brightly painted, alongside a statue of the reigning emperor. At the back of the Chapel, or down some stairs at one side and under an adjoining room, would be the sunken strongroom, where the pay and savings were kept. Some fine examples of such strongrooms have been found at Benwell, Carrawburgh, Bewcastle, Vindolanda, Greatchesters and Risingham, and when excavators reached that at Chesters, they found that the oak door, studded with iron, lay rotting at the entrance to the vault. At Benwell the strongroom, to the east of the Chapel, was cut in the rock and decorated with wall-plaster. Light was provided by a splayed window in its southern wall. A sentry would mount a constant guard over the Chapel.

The Commanding Officer's Residence

On one side of the Headquarters stood the commanding officer's residence (praetorium), a sumptuous courtyard building with its own bath-suite, not unlike a small villa. Commanding officers of auxiliary regiments were usually men of some standing in their own towns of the Roman world, and they expected accommodation in accordance with their rank and social status. They alone were allowed to have their families and servants in residence with them. Little is known of these buildings in Wall forts, although that at Housesteads has been excavated, and in the 1830's Anthony Hedley examined part of the residence at Vindolanda. We can assume, however, that they were well made, provided with good hypocausts, and probably furnished in expensive style, although none has so far produced mosaics. Hadrian had some curt comments to make about ostentatious commanding officers' houses, and in his day there may have been some restrictions.

One of the fort granaries at Housesteads.

Granaries

On the other side of the Headquarters lay the fort granaries (horrea), of which the best examples to be seen lie at Housesteads. On the basis of a normal ration for a soldier of three pounds of bread a day, which is the equivalent of seven hundredweights of grain per man per year, and with a cubic yard of grain weighing 14.5 hundredweights, it follows that half a cubic yard of grain would provide a daily three pound bread ration for one man for a year. According to Roman army practice, a regiment should have storage capacity for one year's supplies, so these granaries must reflect the size of their regiments. At Housesteads there was a garrison of 1,000 men, who would need storage for 500 cubic yards. With 15 feet long wooden bins, 5 feet deep and 5 feet high, the north granary at Housesteads could hold exactly 500 cubic yards of grain in 12 such bins. The south granary could then be reserved for other essential stores, such as wine, beer, cheese, lard, olive oil, salt and fish sauces, together with racks of meat. The external stone buttresses which are an easily recognisable feature of these buildings supported the roof trusses, since the external walls needed louvres in them to allow fresh air to circulate in the building, to reduce the temperature.

Hospitals

The larger infantry battalions and cavalry regiments possessed fort hospitals which would also be found in this central range. It would be a courtyard building, with small wards around all four walls. There would be a small operating theatre, and stores for medical supplies. No doubt it was rarely empty, and the young doctors, often Greek, who had chosen to serve for a few years in the army, must have obtained a great deal of experience in a short time, especially with broken bones. A strength Report from Vindolanda, dating to around A.D.90, recorded that more than 10% of those men present were sick, but not all would have needed hospital treatment.

Workshops

Lastly, the central range might also house a workshop of some kind, probably for the regimental smith or armourer. He would hardly have to operate in the village outside the fort walls, and his forge would have to be kept well away from the barrack area.

A strength report from Vindolanda, circa A.D.90, showing that only a third of the garrison was actually present at the time.

13

Barracks & Stables

The best preserved barrack buildings are at Chesters.

The long narrow buildings in both retentura and praetentura were barracks (centuriae) and stables. Few barrack buildings have been fully excavated, and we need to know more about their internal arrangements, especially to see the extent to which they were developed during Roman occupation. In general terms, the barrack buildings housed a company (centuria) of soldiers and their centurion. The latter lived in a small flat at one end of the building, whilst the troops, divided into groups of some 8-10 men (contubernia), had one small room for each group. How many such buildings one should expect in a fort is still something of a mystery, and whilst it is almost certain that the numerical strength of regiments in the fourth century bore little relation to their paper strength of 500 or 1,000 men it is not certain that the Hadrianic strengths were as they should have been. Professor Birley, however, believes that a cohors milliaria peditata would have ten centuries of 80 infantrymen and 8 troops (turmae) of 30 cavalrymen (1040 men). By the same token, a cohors equitata would have six centuries of 60 men and four troops of cavalrymen 30 strong. These divisions within the regiments would be reflected in the barrack accommodation, and at Vindolanda, when the Fourth Cohort of Gauls, part-mounted, was in occupation, we should expect to find six barracks for the infantry and four for the cavalrymen.

The remaining buildings in the front and rear portions of the fort might be devoted to stables, but we know little of their layout, even in a cavalry fort. It may be that the majority of the mounts were kept out throughout the year, guarded by sentries - at any rate, there would scarcely be enough space within the fort walls for all the animals, except in an emergency. Each regiment must have had up to a couple of hundred oxen, whose main task was to haul the heavy baggage carts.

Water & Sanitation

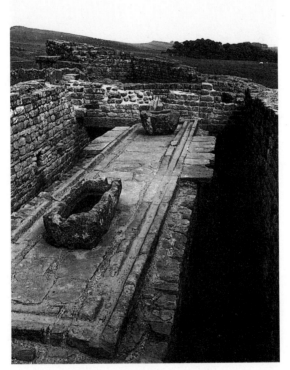

The latrine building at Housesteads - perhaps a 16 seater.

Finally, an important feature of every fort was the water and sanitary system. No fort has been excavated in sufficient detail for us to have a complete plan of a system, but a good deal was revealed at Housesteads. There an aqueduct may have brought water into the fort from the Knag Burn, which would have been dammed at some place, and a pump would be installed to ensure that the fort, higher up the hill, had a constant supply of running water. The construction of aqueducts was regarded as an important task by the garrison, and their completion was sometimes commemorated by an inscription slab, such as that at Chesters, which recorded 'Water brought for the Second ala of Asturians under Ulpius Marcellus, the Emperor's Governor'. Within the forts, increased storage capacity was ensured by the provision of large water-tanks, to trap the rain-water from the eaves of buildings, and to enable the troops to draw their supplies from close to their barracks. The sides of these tanks are often worn-down, as at Housesteads, either by the persistent sharpening of knives and swords, or by vigorous washing of clothes.

A comprehensive drainage system would be laid down before the construction of any buildings within the fort. The latrine-block in the south-east corner of Housesteads is the finest example of such a building in Britain, and it required special supplies of water to flush out the sump and supply the water for the stone channels in which the sponges were washed out. Not all latrines were flushed in this manner, however, and where the necessary water-supplies were unobtainable, leather buckets would have to be positioned beneath the seating, providing an unwelcome chore for the duty troops every day. A latrine block such as that at Housesteads, which could perhaps seat some sixteen men in comfort, may seem small for a regiment of 1,000 men, but there would presumably be the equivalent of Elsans in the barrack blocks as well.

Garrison Duties

At any given time most regiments would be well below their official complement. Our only strength report from Britain detailed the situation at Vindolanda circa A.D. 90, when the First Cohort of Tungrians, commanded by the Prefect Julius Verecundus, reported that of its 761 men, including 6 centurions, no less than 469 of the men and 5 of the centurions were absent, and of the remaining 287, 30 were unfit for duty! In this case a large detachment, of over 300 men, was at Coria or Corbridge for some reason, and others were with the legionary legate, probably at York, acting as his personal guards; another group had gone off to collect the pay; others were in Gaul, but the activities of the remainder can no longer be read on the document. This may not have been a typical scenario, but there were many other reasons for absences. It is clear that the delivery of mail around the country, the collection of supplies from the major stores depots like Catterick, the necessity for reconnaissance patrols or even taking leave would deplete every garrison. But however many men were in residence, there was no shortage of work to be undertaken.

5 cm

Part of a letter from Vindolanda, seeking the return of a decurion to his own cohort.

Guard Duty

Guard duty was a frequent and essential occurrence in the lives of most auxiliaries. The records of the Twentieth Palmyrene cohort at Dura in Syria show that over 20% of the unit strength did guard duty every 24 hours, although its posting in a large town may have necessitated greater watchfulness than usual. But the northern frontier in theory at least should have been equally demanding. The guard commander would have been the duty centurion or his deputy, the optio, and he would have a number of 4 man pickets at his disposal.

During the day, guards manned the fort gates, patrolled rampart walks and probably kept a watchful eye on the unit store park and horse lines. Others were required for sentry duty at the aedes or regimental chapel, and the commanding officer might require one at his own front door. At night additional guards would be needed to patrol the stores parks outside the fort, perhaps accompanied by dogs.

According to Polybius, the day's password would be written down on a wooden tablet and issued to an orderly by the senior officer in charge of the guard: he would then show it to all the guards and return it to the commander. Predictable passwords such as 'palm wreath', 'victory', and 'courage' are recorded, but many must have been more prosaic. The duty officer would inspect the guard at intervals during both day and night, being challenged to produce the password. On paper it sounds an efficient system, but in practise mistakes could occur.

Petty theft must have been the most obvious crime that sentries had to watch for, since a fort and its supplies represented a great temptation to impoverished natives - and to hard up soldiers who might be tempted to raise extra funds by selling military stores to civilians.

The Roman army <u>cornu</u> blower - on whom the soldiers relied for most commands.

Parades

Military parades were of several kinds, varying from the full dress ceremonial review, when the troops wore their special drill uniforms, to the routine sick, punishment and fatigue parades. A full dress occasion would take place on the regimental parade ground near the fort. Little is known about the size or layout of these on the northern frontier, but that at Hardknott fort covered three acres, and there was space at Vindolanda for more than that. They would often be paved or cobbled, with a raised platform (tribunal) for the commanding officer or drill sergeant in the centre or at the side. Altars from Maryport's parade ground suggest that fresh dedications were made every year, with the old altars being buried in deep pits at the side of the paved area.

When a major parade was held, in honour of the Emperor's birthday or for the benefit of a visiting dignitary, hours of spit and polish and days of rehearsal would precede it, but the reward for a good performance might be a holiday or a banquet.

The battalion would show off its battle drill, with the men marching in open and close order, turning to the left and the right, dividing into files and forming squares. Such drills probably reflected the battle tactics of a former age, as is the way of armies.

18

Lorica segmentata, the body armour primarily of legionaries.

The most tedious parade must have been the ordinary morning assembly, held on the roads adjoining the ramparts or perhaps in the courtyard of the Headquarters Building. The Northumbrian moors can be grim on a damp winter's morning, and the fort walls would not offer much protection from gales at exposed forts like Carrawburgh or Housesteads. The parade must have taken at least half an hour, with the calling of the roll and the day's duty rosters being read out. These were presumably all recorded on writing tablets in northern Britain - some have survived at Vindolanda - but in the east a roll of papyrus would have been more convenient. At Vindolanda one tablet lists duties for 343 men, who were despatched to work on building a bath-house, making shoes, collecting lead and rubble, or working in the kilns and clay pits, and plastering some building. The 'immunes', of course, would not appear on these rosters, and they would get on with their normal duties as clerks, medical

Ceremonial facemask from Ribchester, as worn by cavalrymen.

orderlies, armourers or tending the animals.

Training

The foremost task of a commanding officer in peacetime was that of keeping his men in good fighting shape, and training had to be continuous for all. Physical fitness was first assured by a series of exercises approved in military manuals, for, as Fronto pointed out, inactivity was fatal in all walks of life, but especially in the business of war. The soldiers had to endure route marches in full kit: modern scholars are not in agreement over the weight of this, but it was considerable. The weapons and armour probably amounted to 30lbs, and the military pack, containing cooking equipment, food and some spare clothing would probably be at least 40lbs, and perhaps as much as 60lbs. A modern commando is trained to carry a rucksack weighing up to 60lbs, together with his rifle and ammunition, and even with rigorous training such a load is a grievous burden for most men. The Roman soldier was probably stronger, however, since his muscles would be inured to constant physical effort in a manner which no modern soldier can emulate, thanks mercifully to improvements in transport and other civilised labour-saving devices since then. Nevertheless, route marches are basically things to be endured for the good of the army, not to be enjoyed by any but masochistic individuals, and the Roman army went on its route marches with alarming frequency.

A javelin-throwing <u>ballista</u>, usually operated by legionaries.

20

The manuals recommended that the troops be exercised in this manner at least once every ten days. Their pace was not fast, nor could one expect it to be with that load, but they kept it up for hours. The normal military pace worked out at about three miles an hour, and the troops were expected to cover 18 miles in six and a quarter hours, which left little time for halts. The extended pace gave them a range of 22 miles in the same time, that is some three and a half miles an hour. The troops marched in close formation, in step, and their marching songs were of similar content to the modern variety - rhythmical, lively, amusing and unprintable. The roads of the Tyne valley must have been crowded with marching troops, hurling offensive comments at passing bodies from neighbouring battalions, or eyeing the cavalry enviously. Keen eyes must have read the inscriptions on the milestones with more than academic interest in those days.

But much of the training took place on those regimental parade grounds. Vegetius has painted a vivid picture of the scene which must have been a familiar one in northern Britain. The younger soldiers and recruits had two sessions a day, morning and afternoon, on the parade ground, whilst the older soldiers made do with a single session. They exercised at first with dummy weapons, thrusting and slashing at different parts of a target, as in the manner of the old bayonet drill. They appear to have practised this drill while standing still, and then repeated the process on the move, leaping forward to thrust with the weapon, jumping up and down and backwards as well. They also had to practise throwing their weapons at a target, to strengthen their arms. This training had to be maintained throughout the year, regardless of the weather, and to ensure continuity, many units constructed drill halls, or riding schools for the cavalry, within the forts, in front of the Headquarters building. Examples of such buildings in the Wall area have been found at Haltonchesters and Netherby. On the parade ground, too, they would learn the multitude of bugle calls used by the Roman army - calls for meals, for changing the guard, for leaving camp, and for every manoeuvre in battle. The cornu discovered at Pompeii had a range of seventeen notes, and the variety of such calls was therefore considerable. It must have been bewildering for the recruit, but in time a man reacts swiftly to such calls, and they were essential above the din of battle.

It was as important to a Roman soldier as it is to a modern soldier that he was thoroughly proficient with his weapons. The basic exercises described above developed strength, agility and stamina, and the skills now followed. As Vegetius pointed out, they had to learn how to thrust with the sword, and not to slash, since Romans easily defeated men who fought in that manner. A slash cut, however powerfully delivered, rarely killed, according to Vegetius, because the vital parts were protected by the enemy's armour and bones. But a thrust need only penetrate two inches to cause death - if it was made in the right place. And a slashing man leaves himself dangerously exposed to attack from the side, whereas the thruster keeps the body protected by shield and armour. Other refinements, such as the correct way to hold a shield in defence, and how to use its boss to smash into the face of the enemy, were also taught very thoroughly.

Once the individuals had satisfied their drill instructor, they could move on to practise group formations. Dio gave the details of what was perhaps the most famous Roman infantry formation, the testudo. The lightly armed troops were placed in the centre of the group, together with baggage animals and cavalry. The heavy infantry, who used the oblong, curved and cylindrical shields, were drawn up outside them in a rectangle, facing outwards, with their arms at the ready. Their comrades in the inner ranks, carrying flat shields, placed them above their own heads and over those of their colleagues, so that nothing but shields could be seen by the enemy. A hail of missiles would bounce upon only the shields, and the group became, in effect, an armoured mass. Such a manoeuvre obviously had its limitations - it was rather like a tortoise curling up into its shell when small boys threw pebbles at it - but it was effective against long-range arrows or stones, and once the enemy had exhausted its stock of missiles, the tortoise would uncurl and move slowly forward. Dio went on to relate that the overhead cover thus provided by the men with flat shields was so strong that a man could walk across the top of a testudo - and, embroidering his tale a little, that it was a useful manoeuvre when the army came to a steep ravine or ditch, since they could form up in the prescribed manner and allow the horses and wagons to be driven across the obstacle on the roadway created by the shields. A very highly trained unit of selected men might be able to carry out this feat, but it would have been beyond the strength and training of the majority.

Cavalryman with his horse. He received more pay than his infantry colleague.

The training just described applied to the infantry battalions: it goes without saying that the cavalry had just as thorough and strenuous a routine. Cavalry weapons were the shock-lance, carried in the right hand, javelins (carried in a quiver), a long sword, slung on the right side: defensive armour included a shield, slung behind, a breastplate and helmet similar to those worn by infantry. The men would be thoroughly trained and exercised in the use of all weapons, of which the most difficult was the javelin, which had to be thrown while wearing the breastplate at the gallop. Arrian describes how they trained by galloping with the shock-lance forward in the thrusting position and then reversed for the pursuit. Then, wheeling their horses, they had to lift their shields above their heads, place them behind them, whirl the shock-lance round above heads, and chase in mock pursuit of another enemy. Then they drew their swords and went through the motions of slashing at the enemy and finishing off a fallen foe. While the horses recovered their wind the men practised mounting in different ways, before the final exercise of mounting while the horse was at the gallop. Some cavalrymen were armed with slings of one kind or another, and they had to learn how to use them while at the gallop as well.

The troop commander (decurion) was responsible for the training and turn-out of his men and their horses, and he had to ensure that they were intimately familiar with every tactical manoeuvre and bugle call. Inspections would check the cleanliness of the weapons, and a good deal of spit and polish would be required to keep them up to the regulation standard, while the men would have to clean the harness and horse's protective armour to the same standard. The health of the horses was equally important, and spare mounts would have to be groomed, trained and exercised as well.

One exercise, described by Xenophon, was probably used by the instructors in countryside around the forts. Troopers were organised into pairs: in turn each took the role of the fugitive and the pursuer. The fugitive galloped over difficult ground, with his spear reversed, while the other tried to catch him. The pursuer had buttons of leather or wood placed over the sharp points of his javelins, and as soon as he came within range he hurled them at the fugitive. Within striking distance, he hit out with his spear, which was also suitably muffled. He then had to follow the drill for dismounting an opponent, still at the gallop. He had to practise pulling his enemy towards him and then thrusting him hard away, since it was the best way to throw him off his horse. By the same token, the fugitive had to learn how to avoid this tactic, by urging his horse forward at the right moment and thus unseating his opponent. Such exercises on the boulder strewn moors of the Wall area must have taken their toll in broken limbs, for both men and horses, and the fort hospitals would never be empty. But they must have produced a thoroughly proficient cavalryman, for the control of a galloping horse is a difficult enough matter over broken ground when one is carrying a fistful of javelins and a spear, and the absence of stirrups, while preventing a rider from being dragged along the ground if he fell, nevertheless did not make the manoeuvre any easier.

A cavalry horse's chamfron, from Vindolanda.

A reconstruction of the chamfron on a horse's head

Once the cavalrymen were fit and well versed in the handling of both horses and weapons, the unit could proceed to formation exercises, such as the 'tortoise', the 'Petrinos' or the 'Cantabrian'. These required hours of practice by men and horses already well trained in cavalry manoeuvres, and displays were sometimes organised to impress local dignitaries or visiting generals.

Cavalry trained in this manner would shatter any but the most organised and substantial native host, and the deep sweeps into both Brigantia and the territory up to the Forth/Clyde line should have quietened prospective insurgents. But as the Red Indians discovered against equally well drilled American cavalry units, there was still scope for the ambush and the night attack, and the best of regiments could have appalling leaders. Whilst a major battle would prove suicidal to the natives, guerilla warfare in the northern hills and forests must have offered plenty of scope for limited successes.

Manoeuvres

At the head of the list of anti-mutiny measures used by the Roman army stood manoeuvres, a word which still strikes a chord of apprehension and gloom in the hearts of soldiers throughout the world. No doubt it was the same in the Roman army. Commanding officers would summon their subordinates to a series of meetings to draw up a plan and appoint the dates. The plan would often be magnificent, involving the erection of temporary camps in far-away hills, mock attacks on neighbouring units, long route-marches and uncomfortable living conditions. No doubt, too, transport broke down or failed to arrive, supplies went astray, the wrong fort was attacked, and groups of men became lost. Army headquarters at York presumably had to authorise large-scale manoeuvres, for such a realistic approach might be mistaken for something else by natives who were not warned in advance, and some areas would be considered too dangerous. However such operations were disliked by troops, and however badly some of them may have been performed, they did serve a definite purpose: the Roman army was the first to conduct such operations as a regular part of its training, and they impressed foreign observers deeply, as they were designed to do. Josephus pointed out that these peacetime manoeuvres were no less strenuous than actual warfare, and that an apt description of them would be 'bloodless battles', compared with the real thing, which was no more than 'bloody exercises'. That such realistic training had its effect is emphasised by Dio, when he says of Hadrian: "In short, both by his example and his precepts he so trained and organised the entire armed forces throughout the whole Empire that even today the regulations he introduced then are the code of the army. This best explains how for most of his reign he lived at peace with foreign nations, because they saw the Roman state of preparation, and were themselves free from interference and in receipt of money".

Practice camps have been identified in parts of the north - Cawthorn not far from York, has some fine examples, and there are others on Haltwhistle Common to the south of Cawfields milecastle on the Wall. Perhaps a number of the temporary camps in the Borders are the result of manoeuvres rather than campaigns, such as those at Amble, on the east coast north of Newcastle, which may have been used by the cavalry detachments from Risingham and High Rochester during their summer training.

At Burnswark the deserted native hill-fort had been used for artillery practice, and in the course of mock attacks slingers had hurled their acorn-shaped leaden bullets at an imaginary enemy. They were probably supposed to recover their ammunition after such a practice but a number of bullets were lost. That the Roman generals took these manoeuvres seriously is to be expected, and the grumbling or lazy man would soon pay the penalty. Appian records how Scipio Africanus marched his men all over the surrounding plains, and each day made them erect forts and demolish them again, one after another. And he inspected everything personally.

Building Projects

Perhaps in the course of the manoeuvres the men would be exercised in some other practices recommended in training manuals. In the north there was every opportunity for swimming practice, in the sea, rivers and loughs, while thousands of acres of scrubland could be cleared of timber and roads could be thrown across the numerous treacherous bogs just north of the Wall itself. And if the commanding officer could cope with manoeuvres no longer, he could still employ his men on an engineering project, designed to keep their limbs exercised and their minds occupied with serious thoughts. We have little evidence of unusual building projects in the north of England, although any timber building could always be converted to stone, and a turf rampart in a fort could be rebuilt with stone. But in Germany commanders were more ambitious. In A.D. 47 Corbulo used his troops to dig a canal twenty-three miles long linking the Meuse with the Rhine, whilst a few years later the commanders of both German provinces set to with big engineering works. Pompeius Paulinus completed a dam for controlling the Rhine which had been started 63 years before by Drusus, and L. Vetus prepared to build a canal to join the Moselle and the Saone. Perhaps the British commanders were satisfied with the greatest engineering task of all, that of the construction of Hadrian's Wall. The mention of engineering works must have been sufficient to raise thoughts of a mutiny in the minds of the British army by the time they had completed

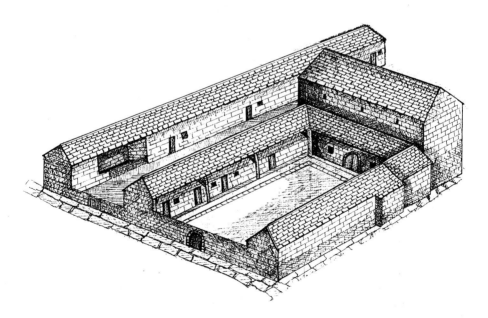

The scope of building projects was enormous - ranging from a <u>mansio</u> or inn for official travellers (as above), to new fort ditches.

the new frontier c.130, and Antoninus Pius was a brave man to order a new Wall in Scotland only nine or ten years later.

Supplies

In such manner the frontier garrison was supposed to maintain its discipline and readiness for action. But there was still much to do before a soldier dared to apply for leave or try to take a few hours off duty in the local village. The army needed its supplies - food, clothing, weapons, fuel and transport.

Roman army marching boots, all heavily studded.

Tacitus claimed that every fort in Agricola's day was provided with sufficient food supplies to last for a year. Such a claim may be doubted, but the huge fort granaries could hold very substantial quantities of the food which both archaeological evidence and Vindolanda writing tablets prove that the soldiers consumed. Corn, meats of all kinds, oil, fish sauces, spices and salt were essential, as was vinegar, Celtic beer and wine. The great concentration of army units in the north was such that the bulk of the supplies had to be brought up from the south or imported from the Continent. Catterick was a major stores depot for the frontier garrison, as the Vindolanda tablets imply, and the port at South Shields and others on the west coast must have had similar roles. But each garrison had its own oxen and horses (and may well have bred from them), together with pigs, chickens, goats and sheep. At Vindolanda grain was supplied to one Lucco 'for the pigs'. Fish was popular, as were oysters. The latter was probably sent inland, in barrels of brine, from the beds on the Solway, but the northern rivers were teeming with fish of many kinds, including salmon. Some units had small groups of men described as 'hunters', responsible for collecting wild game such as deer and boar.

Celtic beer would be produced at each fort in the cervesaria or brewery, and the commanding officer's household consumed great quantities of it at Vindolanda. Wine was imported from Spain, Gaul, Italy and even the Isle of Rhodes, usually in large amphorae.

Clothing was often supplied by civilian contractors, but most of the armour would come from the legionary workshops. Leather would be needed in vast quantities. Tents, ox waggon covers, aprons, trousers, buckets, horseharness, and shoes would consume thousands of ox and goat hides each year. Some may have been tanned locally, but Catterick certainly had an industrial complex devoted to tanning, as early as A.D.120. Once the hides reached the forts, specialists would turn them into the necessary goods, and even amateurs patched up the tents and repaired their own footwear.

Whilst food and clothing were perhaps the most basic of requirements, others were not far behind: timber for building and for fuel, coal and charcoal for heating, bracken, mosses and heather for bedding and carpets; iron and lead for a multitude of tasks, stone for roads and buildings - the list is endless.

Painted inscription on an amphora, containing olive oil from Southern Spain.

Textiles rarely survive, but this sock from Vindolanda is a reminder of what was a major industry in the Roman period.

The army quartermasters controlled a huge variety of stores, as in this list from Vindolanda. Everything was carefully listed, with its price.

Pay and Allowances

Roman small change - bronze coins from Vindolanda.

All of this military activity was rewarded in the form of cash payments at regular intervals. Unfortunately we have only fragmentary and sometimes contradictory information about the wages structure of the Roman Army, and the complications created by inflation during the period of occupation make it impossible to lay down any basic scale. But the pay appears frequently to have been eroded by inflation, leading to many grumbles and even mutiny.

In the mid second century, shortly after the construction of Hadrian's Wall, the pay of the legionary soldier appears to have been 300 denarii a year, paid in three equal instalments at four monthly intervals. Higher grades of legionaries - effectively N.C.O.'s and junior officers - received up to double the legionary pay, as did the centurions. But all that can be said for certain about the auxiliary soldier's pay is that it was less than that of legionaries, and that the cavalry troopers received more than the infantryman.

It is impossible to translate Roman pay into modern currencies, but it is likely that for most of the time the rate of pay was sufficiently attractive to secure a steady supply of recruits. In other words, Roman soldiers were probably paid on a scale broadly equivalent to that of the modern British soldier.

If the Roman soldiers were to receive their full quota of pay, the roads of Britain would have been jammed with waggons loaded with money every four months, presenting a wonderful target for a variety of thieves. In practice, however, the soldiers rarely received more than half of their pay: army stoppages came into effect.

The soldiers had to pay for items of clothing, for weapons and for food - and all too often sweeteners were demanded by centurions for a variety of favours. There also appears to have been a system of compulsory savings, with payments towards funeral

30

An artist's impression of the Roman army in battle - probably a very rare occurrence once the Wall was built.

The austere barracks were the homes of the soldiers, but they were allowed more space per man than in many a modern army.

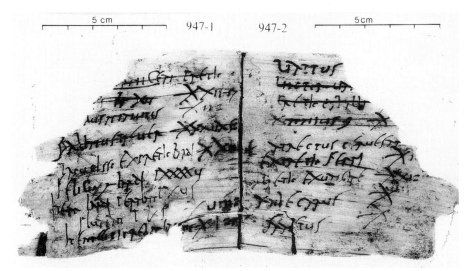

A quartermaster's account from Vindolanda, with some items deleted after payment.

expenses and the like. Many of the Vindolanda documents record the price of Roman army goods dispensed to soldiers, with items ranging from horses to pork fat and boot laces. It is very unlikely that any money actually changed hands on these transactions: it was a book keeping exercise designed to reduce the amount of cash required on pay days.

Many an Emperor wisely gave a donative, or cash present, to the soldiers on his accession, and this would be banked in the Regimental vaults.

Thus the soldiers did have some cash available when opportunities to spend arrived.

Off Duty

There is no doubt at all that an efficient regiment, paying due regard to its military training and the demands for its supplies, would not leave its troops with much spare time. But eventually there had to be some relaxation. Leave was not on the job description of a Roman soldier, but it was sometimes granted, and both papyrus documents from the East and Vindolanda tablets witness the formal applications to the commanding officers for leave (commeatus). How long they were granted is not known, nor where most of them went, but perhaps the large town at Carlisle might offer most scope.

Commanding officers might organise some inter-unit sport, or book a travelling theatre company for a few performances. Tacitus records one such inter-services wrestling competition in A.D.69, between a legionary soldier and a Gallic tribesman, which attracted a large crowd, but he reports that the excessively partisan

Housesteads fort from the north, with traces of the civilian settlement on three sides.

spirit displayed by the supporters of both men spoiled the match. One can picture the scene and its consequences! Tug-of-war, horse racing, gladiatorial combats and athletic contests could be arranged and probably were from time to time. One of the minor mysteries of the northern frontier is the apparent absence of amphitheatres. There must have been some, but they have yet to be discovered - perhaps Corbridge or Carlisle are the most likely sites.

The military bath-house, usually built outside the fort, was much more then a place to sweat out the dirt and be cleansed with fragrant oils. It was the Roman soldiers' equivalent of the British army NAAFI, and the excavation reports from bath-houses in the north show that the troops relaxed in the heated changing rooms with mugs of wine or local beer, played dice or backgammon or draughts and nibbled delicacies. That they gambled is certain: they made offerings to Fortune, the genius of such matters. Their food would consist of specialities which were not part of the normal diet, such as pastries and sweets, and they obviously enjoyed both oysters and mussels.

For those who could afford it, there was hunting in plenty all over the northern hills, though care would have to be taken that such activity did not disturb the uneasy calm of a Brigantian peace. Wild boar roamed the Pennines along with wolves, deer, (larger than the modern breed) and foxes: Gaius Tetius Veturius Micianus, commanding

33

Gladiatorial scene from a glass vessel found at Vindolanda in 1989. No amphitheatre has been found on Hadrian's Wall.

Imported samian ware was probably too expensive for the ordinary soldiers.

Military bath-house at Vindolanda, soon after excavation in 1970. Note the thick layer of plaster on the wall of the apse.

officer of the ala Sebosiana at Binchester dedicated an altar to 'Silvanus the unconquered, for the capture of a boar of exceptionally fine appearance, which many of my predecessors have been unable to take' and he probably used some of his troops as beaters. In a land famous for its hunting dogs, the sport should have been good. Fishing would attract some, and the waters of the Tyne, famed for their salmon in the days before industrial revolution, probably exasperated or thrilled generations of Roman soldiers.

But ultimately commanding officers had to allow their men to choose their own off-duty entertainment, however much they deplored their choice. The villages which grew up beside the forts had much to offer a bored soldier with a little money in his pocket. Appian tells us that Scipio found a large number of traders, prostitutes, seers and fortune-tellers following a Roman army, and Hadrian had to limit the pubs and eating houses outside military establishments. Fronto says that the army of the East in the middle of the second century spent more time in near-by beer-gardens and theatres than in camp, and were frequently drunk and gambling - but the East always seems to have such an effect upon European soldiers. The fault, however, lay with the commanding officers - the men's free time should have been less. Our excavations in the Wall villages show plenty of evidence for shops, inns and gambling establishments.

The modern search for the evidence of civilian settlement.

For many years the Roman army attempted to escape from the consequences of having to cater for the men's families by banning marriage for soldiers - indeed, enlisting into the army was one way of obtaining a divorce, albeit a somewhat drastic method. Some time after A.D.197 these restrictions were lifted, probably when Caracalla gave citizenship to all those living within the borders of the Empire. 'Unofficial' marriages had, of course, taken place, and between A.D.54 and 140 the diplomas issued to men on discharge from the army (honesta missio) had awarded them citizenship and legitimised any children they might have had. But this privilege to the bastard children was stopped in A.D.140 because of the effect it was having upon recruitment to non-citizen units - for the children of recently retired auxiliary-men, as citizens, were eligible for the more attractive legionary service, and on static frontiers this was having a serious effect upon the manpower available for service in the auxilia. After Caracalla's edict in A.D.212 or 213, the soldiers in the auxiliary regiments became citizens overnight, and thus permitted legal marriage. Henceforth, the growth of civilian settlements outside forts could be officially encouraged. There were advantages to Rome in the new system. The responsibilities of marriage perhaps acted as a stabilising factor in the performance of the troops, the soldier was more likely to settle down near his old fort and perhaps farm a few acres, assisting the economic development of the region and the army food suply.

Until the Caracallan decrees, however, the men had recourse to other unions. A man could always purchase a slave girl and live with her. A letter from the legionary Claudius Terentianus, written to his father in Alexandria, in the early second century, illustrates the practice: "Julius sent me word about a woman; he was buying one for me with my approval. As far back as two years ago I would have taken a woman into my house, but I did not permit myself - nor even now - to take one without your approval, and you will not hear otherwise from me on this subject". Few, perhaps wrote home to their parents about it in this way, but many must have adopted the custom. There were always prostitutes for those who did not want a permanent union. Two thousand prostitutes are alleged to have followed the army at Numantia, whilst brothels must have featured in most towns and villages. At Dura an NCO seems to have been responsible for billeting a troupe of about forty actresses or prostitutes, and he put them conveniently into a house only two blocks away from the troops' barracks. A road tariff set up at Coptos in A.D.90 contains a schedule of charges for various categories of people using the road, and prostitutes had to pay five times as much as the second heaviest charge. They obviously had the money.

Punishments

The maintenance of good discipline has always required a clear code of penalties for those who fall below an acceptable standard. In the Roman army the company commanders or centurions were notorious for their use of swagger sticks on lazy men, and a serious offence could result in a severe beating. An unnamed Vindolanda soldier, circa A.D.120, wrote a moving plea for mercy to a senior officer - his own prefect had been detained elsewhere by ill-health - complaining that he had already been lashed with rods until he was covered with blood, and that since he was both innocent and a man from overseas, he should not be treated in this way. This implies both that a second dose of punishment was about to be applied and that there was some distinction between troops from the Continent and those raised from the local population.

Other penalties, often as effective, included loss of privileges - particularly odious to the 'immunes', men excused fatigues - or additional guard duties. The ultimate penalty, rarely used, was that of death, usually carried out in front of the fort wall, when a man's comrades would kill him with stones.

Religion

Religion played a much greater role in the life of the Roman soldier than it does with a modern soldier, for although Training Manuals may still insist that the British Royal Navy believes in God, and a variety of chaplains are maintained on the strength to administer the faith, it would not be true to infer that sailors in general could be classed as religious men. In the Roman world, and in Celtic Britain, men did not have the self-assurance in such matters that modern man adopts, and a great variety of religious dedications testify at least to a superficial show of religious belief. The Roman army permitted freedom of religion, within reason, but it incorporated certain safeguards. There were thus a few official cults whose worship or veneration were obligatory, as well as a wide range of others which were permitted if not actually encouraged.

Regimental esprit de corps was ensured by the cult of the standards, a more advanced practice than that adopted by modern British units with their colours and battle-honours. The legions had their eagles and emblems, and the auxiliaries had their standards, equally venerated, and securely lodged in the central chapel within the Headquarters building of the fort. The regimental bank was often housed in a chamber beneath the chapel, where security was ensured by the presence of a sentry and by the sacred symbols which no soldier cared to defile. Alongside the Standards altars to a number of official Roman deities would stand. Jupiter Optimus Maximus, the war god Mars and the personification of the goddess Victory would often find a place in auxiliary chapels. Others such as Disciplina, Fortuna and Hercules might be found as well, although Fortuna might be more suited to the bath-house, where she could bring good luck to the gamblers. Room would probably be found for a statue to the reigning Emperor, although few traces of such works have survived. One would like to know what happened to the old statue when an Emperor died: perhaps it was carefully buried in a pit, in the manner of old parade ground altars.

Individuals might place a small altar to their favoured god in a niche of their barrack-room wall, or in a small open shrine, such as that found outside the fort gate at Housesteads. In general, one finds many more of these small 'portable' altars than one does the large variety, and some have obviously had painted inscriptions on them, now regrettably lost. The temples would lie outside the fort, probably on the fringe of the village, near the cemeteries. In these unofficial temples the Roman soldier, whether he was an educated commanding officer or a barely literate tribesman from an irregular formation, paid his vows to his god and hoped thereby for success and good fortune.

The cosmopolitan Roman army brought with it to northern Britain a number of cults which were unfamiliar to the natives. Jupiter Dolichenus and the oriental Mithras found a place outside some forts, although the subtleties of the latter would have been beyond the imagination and perhaps the purse of all but wealthy merchants and officers. The excavation of the Mithraic temple at Carrawburgh supplemented the knowledge we

Stone carving of a mother goddess.

Remains of the temple to the Persian sun-god, Mithras, at Carrawburgh.

already possessed of this cult, and the full-scale reconstruction of the temple in the Museum of Antiquities in Newcastle shows in vivid fashion what the third century worshippers at Carrawburgh must have seen. Mithras is known to have been worshipped as far back as 1400 B.C. by Aryan peoples, and the later version of his faith was spread through the western Roman world at the close of the first century A.D. by the XVth legion, returning to the Danube from service in the East. Mithras the unconquered appealed to army officers, and as a god of contract and truth he also appealed, but perhaps with less reason, to the merchants. The social status of Mithraic worshippers probably ensured that his temple was the most ornate, in the interior at any rate, in the village, but the size of its congregation was small, and other temples may be larger. Evidence for Mithraic worship along the lines of the Wall has been found at Rudchester, Carrawburgh and Housesteads, where the temples have been excavated.

The presence of some gods in the north reflects the origin of the parent regiments. Housesteads thus found itself the scene of worship to the German war-god Mars Thincsus and his helpers, the Alaisiagae, whose names, Boudihilla and Friagarbis must have sounded strange to most Latin speakers. The multiplicity of the spelling found in the altars to Veteris testifies to the comparatively humble nature of his worshippers, who were probably the rankers in the unit. The altar to Mars Thincsus, together with a great stone frieze, were set up by a very humble unit of German irregulars (numerus), brigaded with the First Cohort of Tungrians, evidently in the third century. Excavation in 1961 located the probable source of these altars, a small circular shrine, only 13 feet in diameter, with the crudest of walls, which had been erected over the remains of an earlier workshop and a rubbish dump. The quality of the altars contrasts strangely both with the crude little temple and with the known status of the unit that erected them, and they can have had few funds to spare when it was time to build the temple. One wonders how many of them could have read the inscriptions on the stones.

Perhaps the most interesting cults to us were those which the Romans adopted when they came to the northern frontier. Celtic Britain was just as religious as was the Roman world, and although Druidism was exterminated by the Roman army, perhaps because of its human sacrifice which was abhorrent to them, or because its High Priests meddled in politics too much, other cults would be acceptable for adoption rather than destruction, since the power of their gods was of an unknown quantity, and it was better to be safe. In due course some of these Celtic cults won a wide and probably fervent group of supporters. Brigantia, the goddess of the great tribe of the north, was wisely worshipped by many soldiers, whilst nymph goddesses were invoked at numerous sites. Coventina, whose water-shrine at Carrawburgh was patronised heavily, was a typical Celtic deity, guarding springs and wells, with the subsidiary role as goddess of fecundity and maternity. One wonders what the danger was which made her adherents throw her precious altars into the well - unless it was the same hand of destruction which ruined the Mithraeum nearby, and that has been attributed to Christians. Widespread, too, was the worship of Cocidius, whose home seems to have

left:

The magnificent altar to the native British god Antenociticus and to the gods of the Emperors, set up by Aelius Vibius, a centurian of the Twentieth Legion. One of two altars from the little temple in the civilian settlement outside Benwell fort.

right:

One of many small votive altars, dedicated to the Veteres (or variants of that spelling). The soldiers frequently adopted the local gods, as well as continuing to worship the normal Roman deities.

been north of the Wall in Cumbria, perhaps near the fort of Bewcastle, whereas two more northern gods, Maponus and Belatucadros, had a limited appeal. Maponus seems to have been a god of hunting, with subsiduary roles as a deity to music and poetry, both of which were closely associated with hunting when it came to telling the story of the chase around the fires in the evening. Belatucadros, 'Bright Beautiful One', belies his name by being firmly a god of war, and dedications to him have been found at Carvoran, Burgh by Sands, Netherby and Maryport.

Although the Roman world officially became Christian in the fourth century, the army for long remained the bulwark of paganism. There is nothing surprising in this, for Christianity gave little special support for the soldier, and he may have been happier with his tried gods. There are few traces of the new faith in the north: one or two tombstones are suggestive, and Christian monograms are sometimes found on rings or pewter, although that does not indicate that their owners were necessarily Christians. But Christianity had found a home in the north by the fifth century, as the presence of Candida Casa reminds us, and Brigomaglos from Vindolanda may have been an important late fifth century Christian leader.

The Peactime army

That the Roman army was able to maintain a garrison for so long in the north of England was a tribute to the thorough professionalism of its bureaucracy. Recruits were raised, trained, incorporated into existing regiments, supplied with clothing, arms and food, paid in cash and generally kept in a state of tolerable readiness for action. It was not for the soldiers to question why they were there or how long they were to remain. They were paid to carry out the orders of their superiors.

It was an ordered life, and in comparison to that of the civilian population it was a relatively comfortable life. The routine of training, guard duties and maintenance made good sense, and it did provide money to spend in spare time. There would be a host of events which enlivened that routine, about which we have few hard facts but can guess at. The arrival of new recruits, the death of comrades, the departure of one commanding officer and the arrival of his replacement, the exploits of eccentrics and various scandals would add variety in every fort. That is how it is today in an army regiment, and the Roman army was no different. The soldiers carried out the tasks their government set them, and we can only marvel at the astonishing efficiency of that military machine in Roman Britain.

right:

The most exposed of all Wall turret positions, to the east of Carvoran fort, sadly destroyed by the Walltown quarry company.

When soldiers were granted leave, the attractions of Corbridge (above) and Carlisle, the only two large towns nearby, would have been considerable.

43

Further Reading and References

The late Roy Davies was the most perceptive writer on this subject, and his Service in the Roman Army (Edinburgh University Press, 1989), edited by David Breeze and Valerie Maxfield is both articulate and packed with vital references. Anthony Birley's Life in Roman Britain (London, 1968) is still good value as is David Breeze's The Northern Frontiers of Roman Britain (London, 1982). For Roman Britain in general, see S. S. Frere's Britannia (London, 1967 and later editions), and for the construction of the Wall, see the companion volume in this series.

Also available from Roman Army Museum Publications (Carvoran, Greenhead, Northumberland, via Carlisle, CA6 7JB):

Hadrian's Wall - A Personal Guide	£2.95
The Best of Hadrian's Wall	£1.95
Vindolanda's Roman Records	£3.95
Guide to Vindolanda	£1.50
Guide to Roman Army Museum	£1.50
Junior Guide to Vindolanda	£1.50
Eyeopeners (pack of 20) dealing with life in Roman Britain	£3.95
Posters of Vindolanda and the Wall	£0.99
Hadrian's Wall notelets (16 scenes)	£0.25 each

Acknowledgements

The author is grateful to Alison Rutherford for the majority of the photographs, and to Pat Birley and Graham Sumner for the reconstruction drawings.